FRUIT INFl

MW00948188

50+ ORIGINAL FRUIT INFUSED SPA WATER RECIPES TO REVOLUTIONIZE YOUR HEALTH, CLEANSE YOUR BODY AND (IF DESIRED) START LOSING WEIGHT

BY MARTA TUCHOWSKA

All information in this book has been carefully researched and checked for factual accuracy. However, the author and publishers make no warranty, expressed or implied, that the information contained herein is appropriate for every individual, situation or purpose, and assume no responsibility for errors or omission. The reader assumes the risk and full responsibility for all actions, and the author will not be held liable for any loss or damage, whether consequential, incidental, and special or otherwise that may result from the information presented in this publication.

Health Disclaimer:

A physician has not written the information in this book. Before making any drastic changes to your diet and lifestyle, consult your physician/or other health professional, if applicable, first. Fruit infused spa water is a great natural tool for health, natural weight loss and wellness, but the author is not making any claims, and this book should never be a substitute for any professional medical advice. Some of the recipes provided in this book use natural remedies and herbs, that are generally safe for most people, however we recommend you talk to a qualified herbalist, doctor or other health professional, if applicable, before using them, especially if you're pregnant, on medication or lactating. This book was created merely for educational and motivational purposes to inspire mindful self-care and healthy living. We recommend readers do their own research on any natural herbs or supplements they wish to try an get familiar with any possible contraindications.

From the Author

Thank you for purchasing my book, it really means a lot to me. As always, I am very happy to accompany you on your wellness journey.

It is perfectly fine and extremely healthy to become crazy about this amazingly delicious vitamin water. Many spa and wellness centers serve it to their clients to speed up detoxification process that a massage treatment causes. It seems like a VIP treat and some kind of a gods' elixir that "the masses" are not allowed to access.

However, I specialize in bringing wellness and spa culture to the masses; that is, to modern, busy people in the real world. Everyone can prepare fruit infused spa water at home, and contrary to what some people say, it can be done on a budget.

So, let's learn more about it. I am very happy and excited to introduce you to another holistic wellness tool. The reason why I say "holistic" is that the benefits of hydration aided by natural vitamins and minerals not only will do wonders for your body, but also for your mind and even emotions.

"Take care of your body, that's the only place you have to live"- John Rohn

The way I put it- take care of your body and your wellness. The rest will fall into place...

So, let's get started! I hope you will enjoy my spa water recipes and so will your family!

Table of Contents

About Spa Water 9

THIS BOOK IS FOR 11

BENEFITS OF DRINKING FRUIT-INFUSED WATER...... 11

WHAT HAPPENS WHEN YOU ARE DEHYDRATED 14

FRUIT INFUSED WATER AND THE ALKALINE DIET 14

WHAT YOU NEED 15

FRUITS, HERBS AND OTHER INGREDIENTS 16

GENERAL GUIDELINES FOR CREATING YOUR SPA
WATER: 18

ABOUT THE RECIPES 20

RECIPE#1 SUMMER SPA REFRESHMENT 22

RECIPE#2 GREEN ENERGY DETOX 23

RECIPE#3 Sweet Roibosh Mix 24

RECIPE#4 Vitamin C Power 25

RECIPE#5 Pink-Purple Spa With a Twist 27

RECIPE#6 Anti-cellulite 28

RECIPE#7 After Workout 30

RECIPE#8 Super Alkaline 32

RECIPE#9 Tropical 34

RECIPE#10 Mojito Spa Water 35

RECIPE#11 Sweet Dreams! 36

RECIPE#12 Relaxing 37

RECIPE#13 Natural Fat Burner 38

RECIPE#14 Simple Green Minimal Spa Water 39

RECIPE #15 Rosemary Refreshment 40

RECIPE#16 Energy Ice Tea.. 41

RECIPE#17 Oriental Ice Tea 42

RECIPE#18 Water Retention and Cellulite Killer 43

RECIPE #19 Circulation and Energy 44

RECIPE#20 Simple Kiwi and Parsley Water 46

RECIPE#21 Old Blueberries with a Twist...................... 47

RECIPE#22 Cherry Attack 48

RECIPE#23 Pear and Apple Club 49

RECIPE#24 Citrus and Basil Romance 50

RECIPE#25 Beets Spa Water 51

RECIPE#26 Red Grape VIP Spa Water 52

RECIPE#27 Cilantro Summer Refreshment.................... 53

RECIPE#28 Sweet Strawberry...................................... 54

RECIPE#29 Chamomile ChillOut 55

RECIPE#30 Cantaloupe Attack 56

RECIPE#31 Thirsty Family 57

RECIPE#32 Forest Calling...58

RECIPE#33 Gooseberry Delight 59

RECIPE#34 Cranberries Detox.....................................60

RECIPE#35 Thyme Refreshment................................... 61

RECIPE#36 Super Detox... 62

RECIPE#37 White Tea Cucumber Detox.......................... 63

RECIPE#38 Spinach is Awesome! 64

RECIPE#39 Bilberry Weight Loss Team 65

RECIPE#40 Hibiscus Spa Water for Weight Loss 66

RECIPE#41 Green Tea Made Sweet 67

RECIPE#42 Moroccan Spa Mix 68

RECIPE#43 Echinacea Super Strength Water 69

RECIPE#44 Eucalyptus Infusion Water 70

RECIPE #45 Strawberry and Thyme Spa Water 71

RECIPE#46 Polish Kompot Inspired Spa Water (Apples) .72

RECIPE#47 Cucumber & Celery Detox 73

RECIPE#48 Lavender Vanilla Citrus Dream 74

RECIPE#49 Vanilla Beach-Peach Spa 75

RECIPE#50 Melon Spa Water with a Twist 76

RECIPE #51 Kiwi Cilantro Mix 77

RECIPE#52 Carrot Summer Mix 78

CONCLUSION 79

About Spa Water

I am sure that you know that drinking water is good for you as it flushes out toxins and makes your body function at its optimal levels. All diets underline the importance of proper hydration. No need to add anything here. But putting theory into practice can be such a daunting and tasteless task...Some people simply don't like drinking water. Others get tempted to reach out to sodas, colas, energy drinks, artificial juices, or alcohol.

It's normal that human taste-buds are looking for new sensations and they very often crave anything, but not water or any healthy alternatives. Summertime can even make it worse- we get tempted to indulge into cold beer or anything that can quench our thirst now and give us some kind of pleasurable taste.

It's been scientifically proven that sugar is an addictive substance on par with nicotine in cigarettes as well as drugs like cocaine. Sad but truth. Sugar is a legal drug that harms millions of people every day.

As far as I am concerned, I am used to drinking pure water and I drink quite a lot of it. In fact, my friends always tell me that I drink so much water that I could float away.

However, fruit infused water is another experience. I can spice it up with different natural flavors plus I can add more natural vitamins and minerals to my diet. This drink also helped me cut down on coffee and other caffeine drinks that I used to be addicted to and drank in exaggerated amounts.

I know many people who were able quit artificial soft drinks, colas and energy drinks and restore their energy naturally with fruit infused spa water. I even know athletes who use it for their successful workouts.

How did this drink get invented...? To be honest I don't know. But I can tell you that where I am originally from (Poland) it is extremely popular, especially in the summer. The Polish variation of fruit-infused water is called "*kompot*" (one of the easiest words in Polish I guess!). The mode of preparation is different though but the essence remains similar.

So, I can tell you that I pretty much grew up on fruit-infused water. I didn't even know that a drink such as coca-cola existed until I was about 10 years old.

My parents were always more inclined towards a healthy lifestyle and so they were not big fans of artificial sodas, colas, energy drink or whatever you want to call this poisonous c##p. Because this is what it is- a poison that spreads onto your body over years in order to make you gain weight, add more unnecessary calories into your diet and make your body and mind toxic. Those tactics are very often a part of bigger schemes of creating unhappy and unhealthy society.

Now, who wants to join those unhappy and unhealthy, easily manipulated folks?

I am sure that you don't. You are on your **quench for wellness**, and so am I. I choose health. I want to know what I eat and what I drink!

THIS BOOK IS FOR

- Wellness and health enthusiasts
- Those who wish to lose weight and detoxify their bodies
- Spa Lovers
- Those who are interested in wellness on a budget
- Those who are concerned about artificial juices and sodas and their negative impact on our environment
- Those who wish to have more energy and zest for life and lead a balanced, holistic lifestyle
- Those who would like to improve their mental focus and feel emotional wellness as well

BENEFITS OF DRINKING FRUIT-INFUSED WATER

- The main benefit is the same as drinking water: it helps in digestion and transportation of vital nutrients in your body and at the same time helps eliminate waste products
- It improves concentration- the effect of hydration is enhanced by vitamins and 100% natural. This drink should be obligatory at schools, imagine a relief that

many students would experience! They could stay more focused in the classroom

- Weight Loss- spa water is low in calories and, as it was already mentioned provides your body with vitamins and minerals. A recommend for all healthy weight loss programs!

- Helps maintain healthy alkaline balance in your body- drinks like sodas, coffee and alcohol are extremely acidic. Even if you are not interested in following the alkaline diet you will do yourself a great favor by eliminating or at least reducing those unhealthy drinks that are nothing else but an invention of big companies who don't care about consumers' health (in most cases).

- Helps speed up muscle recovery- spa water is recommended before, during and after workouts. There is no need for artificial energy drinks if you can replenish your body naturally.

- Pleasure for your eyes and taste buds- nice natural flavors are a marvelous experience as far as taste is concerned plus the mixture of different ingredients including naturally colored ice cubes (read on!), make spa water something you crave for naturally!

- Natural anti-age treatment- I am sure that you heard beauticians and spa therapists going on about how important it is to hydrate your skin- well, there you go! Spa water is a perfect solution from the inside out. It can be also used as a skin tonic. For example, lemon-cucumber- rosemary water is a great natural skin tonic and refreshment especially recommended for oily complexions.

- Great naturopathic solution for regular internal organs cleanse; by drinking spa water, you take care of your kidneys and cleanse out your colon

- Immune system booster- fruit infused spa water (especially orange, lemon, kiwi and lime) contain natural vitamin C that helps you strengthen your immune system and have more energy

- Speeds up metabolism and helps lose weight

- Is exciting and fun- your imagination is the only limit of what can be done

- Is affordable- you will spend less money than on coffee and energy drinks. It is also much cheaper than going for healthy alternatives such as juicing and blending. This is a perfect "on a budget" solution for the whole family. It is also easy to prepare and a real time-saver.

- Kid friendly- I have been experimenting with different spa waters and introducing my recipes to my little nephew. He loved different colors and flavors. The trick with colored ice cubes (use small amounts of fruits blended with water) really did the job.

- Encourages creativity- there is so much that can be done! I have noticed that kids also like to take part in spa water preparation. Just ask them a question: "hey, what can we do with those 2 lemons, 1 kiwi and a cup of blueberries?" or: "what color do you want your ice cubes?", or: "I bet you can't have mint with your water, show me how you do it!".

It's fun to educate kids to eat and drink healthy! By making them aware of what artificial drinks do to us and exposing them to healthy and natural alternatives full of amazing tastes and flavors, you will do them a great favor!

WHAT HAPPENS WHEN YOU ARE DEHYDRATED

- Toxin accumulation
- Low energy levels
- Poor concentration and focus
- Anxiety and insomnia
- Weight gain
- Inflammation
- Irregular bowel movement
- Moodiness

We don't want to end up there, right...?

FRUIT INFUSED WATER AND THE ALKALINE DIET

These two go hand in hand. Yes! I was really surprised to meet so many people who were eating healthy and alkaline, but, at the same time, were forgetting about the importance of hydration! The rule number one of the Alkaline Diet, and the first tip that I would give to Alkaline newbies is to drink more water and herbal infusions. There is no exception here and fruit infused water is a great tool to give your body more hydration and Alkalinity as well as minerals and vitamins at the same time.

The Alkaline Diet followers usually prefer green smoothies, water, water with lemon juice and very little pure fruit juices (unless diluted with water and in small amounts) as they are concerned about sugars that many fruits contain. Fruit-infused water on the other hand is virtually sugar-free and a great addition to alkaline lifestyle.

WHAT YOU NEED

You don't need any fancy or expensive equipment, so good news here for those who don't want to spend big bucks on juicers or blenders. The basic things that you will need are: big or small jar(s) or glass bottle(s) or glasses. I would also recommend some reusable straws and long-necked spoon or spatula to crush/ press the ingredients to speed up the process of flavor release.

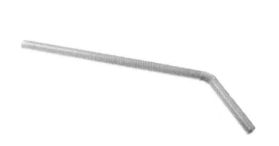

The rest that I list here is optional, as you start experimenting with your spa water, you will find your way and will figure out what makes your life easier:

- Glass pitcher
- Muddler

- Drink strainer-some people like it with "no bits". I have no problem with fruit pieces or some herbs sticking to my teeth (haha!) but it's up to you which option you choose. I am in habit of eating the fruits after drinking my spa water.

FRUITS, HERBS AND OTHER INGREDIENTS

My favorite ingredients include:

- **Fruits and veggies**: Lemons, limes, cucumbers, pineapples, beetroot (yes!), apples, banana, cherries, blueberries, strawberries, cherries, peaches, mangoes, melons, watermelons...

- **Herbs and spices**: cinnamon, mint, lavender, nutmeg, rosemary, basil...

- **Aloe vera water and coconut water**- these are really nutritious and low in calories.

- **Ice cubes**- I always have some in my fridge.

My tip- spice it up with creative and tasty, naturally-colored ice cubs!

THIS IS HOW I DO IT!

Instead of making ice cubs out of old boring H2O, you can also mix it with some fresh fruit juice and have a go with:

- **Blueberry ice cubes**- just blend/ mix a few blueberries with water and freeze them as ice cubes. As they melt in your spa water, it will take a nice hue. A little bit of magic and creativity to spice it up! You can also use beets- the color effect will be amazing!

- **Banana ice cubes** – these will give your water nice and sweet flavor. Kids will love it.

- **Lemon ice cubes**- again, squeeze 1-2 lemons and mix it with water and then freeze; these ice cubes are really alkaline and detoxifying!

- **Kiwi ice cubes**- I have recently made those and had them with my Mojito Water (the recipe is included in this book). It's really impressive as they start melting and your drink goes green. Again- kids love it, and so do old and boring adults! It's a pleasure for your eyes and if you like the way it looks you feel attracted to it (we are humans, it makes sense, right?).

GENERAL GUIDELINES FOR CREATING YOUR SPA WATER:

- You can store your water for about 2 days after it's prepared, in a fridge. You can make more at one go so as to save your time and make sure that you always have some natural refreshments in your fridge. Personally, I never store my water for more than 24 hours, but I have seen others store it for longer.

- Herbs are optional- I love using herbs, especially fresh mint. The general rule is to use more fruits than herbs

- After infusing your fruit in water, store your spa water in fridge for about 1 hour. It will taste better. However, sometimes I am in such a rush that I just make it on a go. I use spatula to press the fruit and add my fruity ice-cubes for special effects!

- Use only good quality filtered water

- Instead of plain water, you can also use aloe vera water or coconut water. I also like to add some cooled green tea (it has some amounts of theine, which is a good thing if you want to quit or reduce coffee and don't want to experience coffee detox headaches). You can also mix water with some cooled roibosh tea or kukicha tea (so alkalizing and delicious!). Roibosh is really sweet while kukicha is bitter, just like green tea.

– ROIBOSH TEA is sweet and super healthy!
– Optional: Add some freshly squeezed lemon or lime juice. I also like to squeeze in some grapefruits or oranges. It gives your water more vitamin C and an amazing color.

ABOUT THE RECIPES

I decided to stick to the measurements that in my opinion are pretty international and easy to understand for readers in different countries. I live in Europe and I am aware that some of you are in North America, Australia or on other continents. I have noticed that different countries use different measurements, and this is why I have decided to simplify things. We already made it too difficult with so many languages and even varieties within the same language. Life is already complicated enough, so let's make it simple.

Ok, back to recipes:

Just in case:

- 1 liter (or: "litre" in British/Canadian and Australian English.)is 33.814 US oz. and 4.22675 cup
- 1 liter is 1 US quart, or: 4 cups
- 1 cup is 0.236588 liter

These may be useful to you if you got other spa water recipe books and are comparing them to mine or you want to combine my recipes with what you read in other books.

Other measurements, as for example "1 cup" are just to get general proportions. Spa water recipes are not like for example baking recipes where one should stick to more precise measurements in order not to mess things up.

****

1 liter of spa water should make 4 cups which is 4 servings.

If you wish to make more than 1 liter, double the ingredients accordingly.

Feel free to transform your recipes. This is what they are for-
they should inspire you to create your own way. I am sure that
some of the ingredients are already in your kitchen!

RECIPE#1 SUMMER SPA REFRESHMENT

SERVES-4

INGREDIENTS

- 5 cucumber slices
- 3 pineapple slices, cut into smaller chunks
- Half cup of watermelon chunks
- A few mandarin pieces cut in halves
- A few fresh or dried mint leaves
- 1 liter of water
- A few ice cubes (I recommend blueberry water ice cubes for "special color effects" and healthy flavanoids that blueberries contain)

INSTRUCTIONS

1. Using a jar/water pitcher/container, mix 1 liter of filtered water with cucumber slices (with skin), pineapple and watermelon chunks and a few small mandarin pieces.
2. Mix well with a spatula and press the fruits for more flavors.
3. Add some mint and store in a fridge for about 1 hour.
4. Serve with a few ice cubes and pour into glasses.
5. Garnish each glass with a slice of lemon.

Enjoy!

RECIPE#2 GREEN ENERGY DETOX

This amazing spa water is also infused with green tea and is great for detox and fat burn. Skip green tea if you are caffeine/theine sensitive (use rosemary or roibosh infusion instead).

SERVES-5

INGREDIENTS

- 1 cup of cooled green tea (use 2 teabags)
- Half banana cut in small chunks
- A few cucumber slices
- 2 tablespoons of dried rosemary
- 1 liter of water
- Juice of one lemon
- 10 strawberries, sliced
- A few ice cubes (I suggest you blend water with some fresh citrus juice, for example grapefruit in 1/1 proportions and freeze into ice cubes, if not- use "normal" ice cubes.)

INSTRUCTIONS

1. Using a jar/ water pitcher/ container, mix water + green tea + fresh lemon juice.
2. Add cucumber slices, banana and strawberries.
3. Use a long-necked spoon or spatula to slightly press the ingredients against jar's wall to mix better. Add rosemary and place in a fridge for about 1 hour.
4. Add a few ice cubes and garnish each glass with a slice of lime or lemon. Grapefruit is also miraculous!

Enjoy!

RECIPE#3 Sweet Roibosh Mix

Amazing, theine-free, herbal infusion spa water full of iron and magnesium!

SERVES-5

INGREDIENTS

- 1 cup of cooled roibosh infusion (use 2-3 teabags if you want a more natural, sweet taste)
- Ginger, peeled. Cut into a few small pieces that resemble the size of a garlic clove. Use 5-8 of those tiny pieces.
- 2 kiwis, sliced
- 2 lemons, sliced
- A few leaves of fresh mint
- 1 liter of water
- A few ice cubes (I suggest you use blueberries for special effect. You can also mix blueberries with water and then freeze into ice cubes!)

INSTRUCTIONS

1. Using a jar/ water pitcher/ container, mix water with roibosh infusion.
2. Add ginger, kiwis and lemons. Spice up with some mint.
3. Stir with a spatula and press the ingredients slightly (more flavor!)
4. Place in a fridge for about 1 hour.
5. Add blueberry ice cubes (or plain water ice cubes, it's up to you).
6. Garnish with fresh mint and enjoy!

RECIPE#4 Vitamin C Power

This spa water recipe is packed with vitamin C and will help you strengthen your immune system! Banana and coconut water make perfect balance with citrus taste.

SERVES-6

INGREDIENTS

- 1 liter of water
- Juice of 2 lemons
- 2 oranges, sliced
- 2 kiwis, sliced
- 2 cups of coconut water (if you can't get any, you can skip this ingredient and use some roibosh infusion or simply add 1 tablespoon of raw organic honey)
- 1 banana, sliced
- Ice cubes- I suggest banana ice cubes here

How to make banana ice cubes:
Blend 1 banana + 1 cup of water. Distribute in an ice cube mold and freeze. Enjoy!

INSTRUCTIONS

1. Squeeze fresh juice of 2 lemons and, in a jar/ water pitcher/ container, mix with water.
2. Add sliced kiwis, oranges and banana.
3. Add some coconut water and/or organic raw honey (1-2 tablespoons).
4. Stir energetically and press the ingredients with a spatula or a spoon.

5. Place in a fridge for about an hour and serve with a few ice cubes.

6. Enjoy!

RECIPE#5 Pink-Purple Spa With a Twist

This spa water is real pleasure both for your taste buds as well as for your eyes! The pink mixes with green!

SERVES-8

INGREDIENTS

- 2 liters of water
- half cup of strawberries, sliced
- half cup of blueberries
- half cup of raspberries
- A few ginger chunks (make them the size of garlic cloves)
- 2 tablespoons of chopped parsley
- 1 cucumber, sliced
- A few ice cubes, I recommend you blend 1 kiwi with a cup of water and turn this blend into green ice cubes!

INSTRUCTIONS

1. Using a jar/ water pitcher/ container, combine water with strawberries, blueberries, raspberries and ginger.
2. Add cucumber slices and parsley.
3. Stir and press the ingredients with a spatula.
4. Place in a fridge for about 1 hour.
5. Serve with some kiwi-green ice cubes.
6. Enjoy!

RECIPE#6 Anti-cellulite

If you suffer from water retention, cellulite, feel bloated and your body feels heavy (water retention symptoms tend to increase in high temperatures) this is the perfect, natural drink for you. Avoid sugar drinks, coffee, energy drinks and sodas at all costs. Turn to nature, it will provide you with more sustainable solutions.

SERVES-6

INGREDIENTS

- 1 cup of horsetail infusion, cooled down (use 2 teabags to make it)
- 1 liter of water
- Half cup of blueberries
- 2 apples, sliced
- A few leaves of fresh mint
- 1 cup of aloe vera water (optional)
- 1 grapefruit, sliced
- A few ice cubes:
  - if you could make them lemon or grapefruit juice infused, you would add to alkalizing effect of this spa water
  - you can also make green tea ice cubes- this will add to fat burning properties of this recipe

INSTRUCTIONS

1. Using a jar/ water pitcher/ container, mix water with horsetail infusion and aloe vera water.
2. Add blueberries, apples and grapefruit.

3. Spice up with some fresh mint and stir well using a spatula or a big spoon. Press the ingredients.

4. Cool down in a fridge.

5. Add a few ice cubes of your choice!

RECIPE#7 After Workout

I love this herbal water after strenuous workouts. I really recommend it for muscle recovery. Not only does it hydrate your system but it is also full of minerals. It tastes a bit like ice tea! Try it yourself!

SERVES-6

INGREDIENTS

- 1 cup of kukicha tea (I suggest you make it stronger, like 2 teabags)
- 1 liter of water
- 1 cup of coconut water
- 2 watermelon slices, cut in small chunks
- A few lime slices
- 1 tablespoon of raw organic honey
- 1 teaspoon of dried rosemary
- 1 banana, sliced
- Ice cubes of your choice (I love banana ice cubes with this one, but it's up to you, as you can see spa infused water can be lots of fun!)

INSTRUCTIONS

1. Using a jar/ water pitcher/ container, mix kukicha tea with water and coconut water.
2. Add watermelon and banana.
3. Spice up with some rosemary herb and lime slices.
4. Add 1 tablespoon of organic honey and stir energetically.
5. Press the ingredients with a spoon or spatula.

6. Place in a fridge for 1 hour or more.

7. Serve with some creative ice cubes of your choice.

8. Garnish with a slice of lime.

9. Enjoy!

RECIPE#8 Super Alkaline

If you are interested in Alkalinity, this is the recipe for you to try. I really recommend it when you suffer from low energy levels or wish to detoxify after a drinking night (it's great for hangover, you can also drink it before you go out in order to hydrate your body and prevent hangover a day after). Alcohol is extremely acidifying, we all know it- this recipe can help restore balance. Of course, I am not saying that you can go drinking with no limits now as you have just found the cure. I am just saying that if it happens, you can use my super Alkaline spa water to restore balance.

SERVES-5,6

INGREDIENTS

- 1 liter of water
- 2 watermelon slices, cut into small chunks
- Fresh juice of 3 cucumbers (you will need a juicer, if you don't have one, you can simply blend a few cucumber slices with 1 cup of water, even a hand blender can handle it)
- A few slices of mint (unless it reminds you too much of endless mojitos you had last night, hahaha!)
- 2 peaches
- A few parsley leaves
- Juice of 2 lemons
- 1 orange, sliced

INSTRUCTIONS

1. Using a jar/ water pitcher/ container, mix water with fresh cucumber juice and lemon juice.

2. Add watermelon, mint, peaches, parsley and orange.

3. Stir gently and press the ingredients.

4. Let it cool in a fridge (for at least 1 hour)

5. Serve with ice cubes of your choice; grapefruit ice-cubes would be awesome!

RECIPE#9 Tropical

Another refreshing option for the summer! You don't need to vacation over in exotic locations to experience the energizing power of this tropical spa water...

SERVES-5

INGREDIENTS

- Half mango, chopped into small pieces
- 1 cup of coconut water
- 1 banana, sliced
- 2 limes, sliced
- 1.5 liter of water
- Optional: a few mint leaves (Personally I love mint, as I said I grow some in my garden and I use it with most of my recipes, but I will leave it to you, I don't want you to think that spa water is only about mint, I am just showing you my way).

INSTRUCTIONS

1. Using a jar/ water pitcher/ container, mix water with coconut water.
2. Add banana, mango and limes. *Optional: add fresh mint leaves*
3. Let cool down in a fridge for about 1 hour.
4. Add a few ice cubes of your choice. How about kiwi ice cubes...? Again, it's up to you. Create whatever suits you and your preferences.
5. Enjoy!

RECIPE#10 Mojito Spa Water

If you throw a party, it's also a good idea to prepare some non-alcohol drinks for your guests. I am sure they will love this one!

SERVES-8,9

INGREDIENTS

- 2 liters of water
- 5 limes, sliced
- 2 tablespoons of cane sugar (optional) or organic honey
- 4 melon slices, cut into small chunks
- 1 cup of fresh mint (oh yea, mint again!)
- Optional- a few leaves of yerba buena
- 1 cup of aloe vera water

INSTRUCTIONS

1. Using a jar/ water pitcher/ container, mix water with aloe vera water.
2. Add melon, limes and fresh mint + yerba buena.
3. Add cane sugar or organic honey and stir energetically.
4. Place in a fridge for about 1 hour.
5. Serve with a few creative ice cubes. My recommendation: freeze some orange juice mixed with water. These will be excellent vitamin C ice cubes and will give your mojito water an incredible taste. I bet that your guests will prefer this alcohol-free drink over real mojitos and other alcoholic beverages!

RECIPE#11 Sweet Dreams!

If you tend to suffer from insomnia or nervousness, this herbal spa water should be your regular afternoon and evening drink. Forget about caffeine and drinks with added sugar.

SERVES-5

INGREDIENTS

- 1 cup of melissa infusion (use 2 teabags)
- 1 liter of water
- Half cup of sliced strawberries
- 2 tablespoons of dried lavender
- 2 oranges, sliced

INSTRUCTIONS

1. Using a jar/ water pitcher/ container, combine water with melissa infusion.
2. Add oranges, strawberries and lavender.
3. Stir and press with a spoon.
4. Cool down. Serve with ice cubes of your choice.

RECIPE#12 Relaxing

Another soothing recipe-perfect after a stressful day!

SERVES-4

INGREDIENTS

- 1 liter of water
- 2 tablespoons of chamomile herb
- 2 tablespoons of dried mint
- 2 cinnamon sticks
- 2 apples, sliced
- 1 banana, sliced
- 1 tablespoon of organic, raw honey
- A few strawberries

INSTRUCTIONS

1. Bring 1 liter of water to boil. Once boiling, add chamomile and mint, turn the heat off and cover. Throw in some cinnamon sticks for flavor.
2. Let it cool down a bit.
3. In the meantime, wash, peel and slice the fruits.
4. Add the fruits to warm, but not boiling infusion.
5. Cover and let it cool down. Add a few ice cubes of your choice. You can have it warm as well. Warm drinks can also soothe the nerves!

RECIPE#13 Natural Fat Burner

Chinese red tea is a famous, natural fat-burner. The problem is that I can't stand its taste. This is why I came up with this recipe- I get to enjoy red tea benefits and amazingly refreshing and tasty drink as well!

SERVES-5

INGREDIENTS

- 1 cup of red tea (use 2 teabags)
- 1 liter of water
- Half cucumber, sliced
- A few pineapple slices, cut into small chunks
- 2 big red apples, sliced
- 1 tablespoon of organic honey or stevia to sweeten, if needed
- A few Ice cubes of your choice-I suggest kiwi or banana!

INSTRUCTIONS

1. Using a jar/ water pitcher/ container, mix water with red tea.
2. Add cucumber, pineapple and apples.
3. Let cool down for at least 1 hour.
4. Serve with kiwi and/or banana flavored ice-cubes.

RECIPE#14 Simple Green Minimal Spa Water

Easy, quick and detoxifying!

SERVES-4

INGREDIENTS

- 1 liter of water
- 1 kiwi, sliced
- 1 banana, sliced
- 1 tablespoon of dried parsley
- 1 tablespoon of dried rosemary
- A few ice cubes of your choice

INSTRUCTIONS

1. Mix all the ingredients in a jar, water pitcher or container.
2. Stir and press.
3. Cool down for at least 1 hour.
4. Add a few ice cubes and serve!
5. Enjoy!

RECIPE #15 Rosemary Refreshment

Rosemary infusion has antioxidant and alkalizing properties. I love warm rosemary infusions in winter, but in summer, I prefer this refreshing recipe!

SERVES-8

INGREDIENTS

- 1 cup of really strong rosemary infusion (use 2-3 teabags)
- 2.5 liters of water
- 2 peaches, sliced
- 2 apples, sliced
- A few dried rosemary leaves or mint leaves
- Surprise blueberry ice cubes; here is how I make them:
  - Mix water with freshly squeezed orange (or lemon or grapefruit) juice (1/1 proportions)
  - Pour in ice cube molds and put 2-3 blueberries in each mold
  - Freeze! These ice cubes are really amazing, as they melt in your water, blueberries are released! Enjoy!

INSTRUCTIONS

1. Using a jar/ water pitcher/ container, mix water with rosemary infusion.
2. Add sliced fruits and rosemary leaves.
3. Stir gently and press the fruits.
4. Cover and cool down in a fridge for about 1 hour.
5. Serve with amazing blueberry ice cubes. Enjoy!

RECIPE#16 Energy Iced Tea

This is a must-do recipe for all those who can't live without iced tea.

There are 2 options here, you can use traditional black tea (I like to have it from time to time), or theine free black tea (I recommend it if you are caffeine/theine sensitive).

This recipe is a natural diuretic.

SERVES-8

INGREDIENTS

- 1 cup of black tea (use 1-2 teabags)
- 2 liters if water
- Juice of 2 lemons (black tea is acidic and lemon juice helps alkalinize it a bit; it's all about balance, right?)
- 1 grapefruit, cut in chunks
- A few slices of pineapple, chunked
- 2 tablespoons of organic raw honey
- A few ice cubes of your choice, how about...mint ice cubes for more refreshment?

INSTRUCTIONS

1. Using a jar/ water pitcher/ container, mix water with black tea and fresh lemon juice.
2. Add grapefruit and pineapple chunks.
3. Add honey and stir. Press the fruits.
4. Cover and place in a fridge to cool down for about 1 hour.
5. Serve with some creative ice cubes and enjoy!

RECIPE#17 Oriental Iced Tea

I love chai tea! It's a really nice guest in my herbal fruity spa waters!

SERVES-5

INGREDIENTS

- 1 cup of chai tea (use 1-2 teabags)
- 1 liter of water
- Half cucumber, sliced
- 1 banana, sliced

INSTRUCTIONS

1. Using a jar/ water pitcher/ container, mix chai tea with water.
2. Add sliced cucumber and banana. Stir and press.
3. Cover and place in a fridge to cool down.
4. Serve chilled and add ice cubes. I like blueberry ice cubes with this one!
5. Enjoy! I love this drink when writing! I find the amazing oriental scents really inspiring and energizing.

You can also make your own chai tea. Simply mix black tea with cardamom, clove, black pepper, cinnamon, and ginger.

RECIPE#18 Water Retention and Cellulite Killer

This recipe is a great complementary drink to support weight loss and cellulite programs. It's also great to help you feel...just lighter and more energized!

SERVES-5

INGREDIENTS

- 1 cup of fennel infusion, cooled (use 2 tea bags per cup)
- 1 liter of water
- 2-3 pineapple slices, chunked
- A few small ginger chunks (peeled)
- Half grapefruit, in small chunks
- 2 apples, sliced
- Optional: a few mint leaves or/and fennel leaves
- A few ice cubes (how about experimenting with kiwis this time?)

INSTRUCTIONS

1. Using a jar/ water pitcher/ container, mix fennel infusion with water.
2. Add fruits and herbs.
3. Stir and press the ingredients.
4. Cover and place in a fridge.
5. Serve chilled and add some ice cubes, enjoy!

RECIPE #19 Circulation and Energy

If you suffer from water retention, sluggish circulation, and cellulite, I have another amazing recipe for you. This one is great if you are pressed for time, or you have some unexpected guests come over. Just make sure you have some frozen blueberries in your fridge!

SERVES-5

INGREDIENTS

- 1 cup of frozen blueberries
- 1 cup of aloe vera water
- 1 liter of water
- 1 lime, sliced
- 1 cucumber, sliced
- 1 lemon, sliced
- Ice cubes
- Optional- 2 tablespoons of dried thyme

INSTRUCTIONS

1. Using a jar/ water pitcher/ container, mix water with aloe vera water.
2. Add fruits and frozen blueberries.
3. Throw in some thyme, stir, and press.
4. Add a few ice cubes of your choice (I would suggest lemon water ice cubes that have a couple of blueberries in them).
5. Cover and place in a fridge. If you are pressed for time or have some unexpected guests, it's OK to cool it down for 15- 20 minutes only. The ice and frozen blueberries will do the trick!

6. Before serving, squeeze in some lemon or lime juice (1 lemon or lime) and add a few more magic ice cubes. Your guests will love it (and love you!) and will ask you for the recipe for sure!

RECIPE#20 Simple Kiwi Water

When it comes to spa water recipes, parsley is very often overlooked...Most people go for mint. But, if you want to add more variety to your recipes, try adding some parsley!

SERVES-8

INGREDIENTS

- 2 liters of water
- 1 cucumber, sliced
- Half cup of parsley
- 4 kiwis, sliced
- A few ice cubes of your choice (hmm...how about strawberry ice cubes? The color and flavor effect will be spectacular!)

INSTRUCTIONS

1. Using a jar/ water pitcher/ container, mix water with kiwis, parsley, and cucumber.
2. Stir and press.
3. Cover and put in a fridge (for at least 1 hour).
4. Serve with a few ice cubes of your choice.
5. Enjoy!

RECIPE#21 Old Blueberries with a Twist

If you can, try adding some coconut water to your spa water recipes. Just be sure to avoid coconut water with added sugar.

SERVES-5

INGREDIENTS

- 1 cup of blueberries (can be frozen)
- Half cup of little ginger chunks (peeled)
- A few mint leaves
- 2 cinnamon sticks
- Optional: 1 cup of coconut water
- Juice of 2 limes
- Ice cubes
- 1 liter of water

INSTRUCTIONS

1. Using a jar/ water pitcher or other container, mix water (+ coco water) with blueberries and ginger chunks.
2. Stir and press.
3. Add mint and cinnamon sticks.
4. Squeeze in 2 limes.
5. Cover and let cool down in a fridge (1 hour or more).
6. Serve with a few ice cubes for special effects!

RECIPE#22 Cherry Attack

Cherries are full of antioxidants and blend very well with ginger!

SERVES-4

INGREDIENTS

- 1 cup of cherries (I recommend pitted)
- 2 slices of watermelon, chunked
- A few slices of ginger
- 1 liter of water
- 2 tablespoons of dried rosemary herb
- A few ice cubes to spice it up

INSTRUCTIONS

1. In a jar, water pitcher or container, mix water with cherries, watermelon, and ginger.
2. Add rosemary. Stir and press the ingredients.
3. Cover and cool down in a fridge.
4. Serve with a few (or more) ice cubes. I suggest cherries or berries!
5. Enjoy!

RECIPE#23 Pear and Apple Club

I love pears! They remind me of my aunt's garden where I would play with my cousins. At the end of August, the end of summer was approaching, and we would be collecting pears and using them for cakes, desserts, and pear-infused water!

SERVES-4

INGREDIENTS

- 1 liter of water
- 2 apples, sliced
- 2 pears, sliced
- A few leaves of mint or rosemary
- 1-2 cinnamon sticks
- A few ice cubes

INSTRUCTIONS

1. Using a jar/ water pitcher/ container, mix water with apples and peaches.
2. Stir and press. Add some mint and/or rosemary.
3. Cover and cool down.
4. Serve with some fresh ice cubes.
5. Enjoy!

RECIPE#24 Citrus and Basil Romance

This spa water has a nice intriguing taste!

SERVES-4

INGREDIENTS

- 1 liter of water
- 1 orange, sliced
- 1 lime, sliced
- 1 grapefruit, sliced
- ¼ cup of fresh basil leaves

INSTRUCTIONS

1. Using a jar/ water pitcher/ container, mix water with fruits and basil.
2. Stir gently and press.
3. Cover and place in a fridge for 1 hour (citrus fruits are fast to infuse so it can be less than 1 h, see what works for you).
4. Serve with some nice ice cubes.
5. Enjoy!

RECIPE#25 Beets Spa Water

I know it sounds horrible, but it is actually delicious! Try it yourself!

SERVES-4

INGREDIENTS

- 2 beets, sliced
- Half cup of cherry tomatoes, sliced
- 2 kiwis, sliced
- Fresh mint leaves
- 1 liter of water

INSTRUCTIONS

- Using a jar/ water pitcher/ container, mix water with tomatoes, beets, and kiwis.
- Add some mint, stir, and press.
- Cover and let cool down for a few hours.
- Serve with some fresh lime or lemon juice and a few ice cubes of your choice. Enjoy!

RECIPE#26 Red Grape VIP Spa Water

If you have some friends over and you want to enjoy a few glasses of wine, it's also good to have some healthy soft drinks at hand.

This one is one of my favorites, and all my friends love it!

SERVES-4

INGREDIENTS

- 1 liter of water
- 1 cup of red grapes
- 1 tablespoon honey
- 2 lemons, sliced
- A few basil leaves

INSTRUCTIONS

1. Using a jar/ water pitcher/ container, mix water with grapes and lemons.
2. Add honey and basil.
3. Stir and press.
4. Cover and cool down in a fridge for a few hours.
5. Serve with a few ice cubes.
6. Enjoy!

RECIPE#27 Cilantro Summer Refreshment

This recipe is very quick and a really powerful antioxidant.

SERVES-4

INGREDIENTS

- 1 liter of water
- 2 peaches, sliced
- A few fresh cilantro leaves
- 1 lemon, sliced

INSTRUCTIONS

1. Using a jar/ water pitcher/ container, mix water with peaches and lemon slices.
2. Add cilantro, stir, and press.
3. Cover and cool down for at least 1 hour.
4. Serve with your chosen ice cubes. How about...blueberries again? Or maybe grapefruit ice cubes? Your imagination is the only limit to what can be achieved.

RECIPE#28 Sweet Strawberry

This recipe is going to satisfy your sweet tooth!

SERVES-4, 5

INGREDIENTS

- 1 liter of water
- 1 cup of sliced strawberries
- 1 lemon, sliced
- 1 lime, sliced
- 2 tablespoons of natural, raw vanilla extract or 2 tablespoons of agave syrup

INSTRUCTIONS

1. Using a jar/ water pitcher/ container, mix water with sliced fruits.
2. Add vanilla and agave.
3. Stir and press.
4. Let cool down for a few hours.
5. Serve chilled with ice cubes of your choice.
6. Enjoy!

RECIPE#29 Chamomile Chill Out

Chamomile adds a nice relaxing smell and flavor to this recipe!

SERVES-4

INGREDIENTS

- 1 liter of water
- 1 cup of blueberries
- ¼ cup of dried chamomile leaves
- 1 grapefruit, sliced

INSTRUCTIONS

1. Using a jar/ water pitcher/ container, mix water with blueberries and grapefruit slices.
2. Add chamomile.
3. Stir and press gently.
4. Let cool down for at least 1 hour.
5. Serve with some fresh lemon juice and ice cubes, enjoy!

RECIPE#30 Cantaloupe Attack

Another easy and quick recipe!

SERVES-8

INGREDIENTS

- 2 liters of water
- Half cantaloupe, chunked
- 1 lemon, sliced
- A few rosemary or mint leaves

INSTRUCTIONS

1. Using a jar/ water pitcher/ container, mix water with cantaloupe chunks.
2. Add sliced lemon and mint (or rosemary).
3. Stir, press, and cover to let it cool down.
4. Serve with some magic ice cubes.
5. Enjoy!

RECIPE#31 Thirsty Family

This is a quick recipe for a thirsty crowd!

SERVES-12

INGREDIENTS

- Half cup of mint
- 1 mango, chunked
- 3 liters of water
- Ice cubes of your choice
- 2 kiwis, sliced
- 2 apples, sliced

INSTRUCTIONS

1. Using a jar/ water pitcher/ container, mix mango chunks with water.
2. Add other fruits and herbs, stir, and press.
3. Cover and cool down in a fridge for a few hours.
4. Spice it up with some super cool and original ice cubes. Now you know what this art is all about!

RECIPE#32 Forest Calling

This is a great recipe for all forest fruit lovers!

SERVES-8

INGREDIENTS

- 2 liters of water
- half cup of redcurrants
- half cup of blackcurrants
- half cup of white currants
- A few leaves of rosemary and mint

INSTRUCTIONS

1. Using a jar/ water pitcher or container, mix water with redcurrants, blackcurrants and redcurrants.
2. Add a few rosemary and mint leaves, stir, and press the ingredients gently against the jar.
3. Cover and let cool down for a few hours.
4. Serve with ice if you want!
5. Enjoy!

RECIPE#33 Gooseberry Delight

If you can find gooseberries (depends on your geographical location), try this recipe! Alternatively, use any other kind of berries.

SERVES-4

INGREDIENTS

- 1 liter of water
- half cup of gooseberries
- 1 apple, sliced
- 1 tablespoon of organic honey, or stevia to sweeten (optional)

INSTRUCTIONS

1. Using a jar/ water pitcher/ container, mix water with gooseberries and apples.
2. Add some organic honey, stir, and press.
3. Cover and cool down for a few hours.
4. Serve with ice cubes if you wish. You can use honey to make it sweeter or lemon juice to make it sour.
5. Enjoy!

RECIPE#34 Cranberries Detox

This recipe is a great, natural source of vitamin C and antioxidants. Plus, it tastes pretty exotic and is very refreshing!

SERVES-4

INGREDIENTS

- 1 cup of cranberries
- 2 limes, sliced
- 2 slices of pineapple, chunked
- 1 liter of water
- A few ice cubes of your choice

INSTRUCTIONS

1. Using a jar/ water pitcher/ container, mix water with cranberries.
2. Add limes and pineapple chunks.
3. Stir, press, and cover.
4. Cool down in a fridge for a few hours.
5. Add a few crazy ice cubes (blueberries ice cubes or even cranberries!) to spice up.
6. Enjoy!

RECIPE#35 Thyme Refreshment

This drink is really helpful for people who are prone to colds and would also like to strengthen their immune systems.

SERVES-5

INGREDIENTS

- 1 cup of thyme infusion (use 1-2 teabags per cup)
- 1 liter of water
- A few rosemary leaves
- 2 kiwis, sliced
- 2 lemons, sliced
- 2 tablespoons of organic honey or royal jelly

INSTRUCTIONS

1. Using a jar/ water pitcher/ container, mix water with thyme infusion.
2. Add kiwis, lemons, and rosemary.
3. Add some honey, stir, and press the ingredients.
4. Cover and place in a fridge for 1-2 hours.
5. For more immune system strengthening effects, serve with some fresh lemon juice. Sour is nice! Enjoy!

RECIPE#36 Super Detox

Have you ever tried white tea before? It's theine free and works as a natural antioxidant. I know that it's good for me, but I find it a bit tasteless. This is why I decided to incorporate it into my spa water rituals! Try it yourself!

SERVES-5

INGREDIENTS

- 1 cup of white tea (use 2 teabags)
- 1 liter of water
- 2 limes, sliced
- 2-3 watermelon slices, chunked
- A few leaves of fresh mint

INSTRUCTIONS

1. Using a jar/ water pitcher or container, mix white tea with water.
2. Add lime slices and watermelon chunks.
3. Spice up with some mint.
4. Stir, press a bit, cover, and store in a fridge.
5. Try in a few hours! Add some ice cubes to spice it up.

RECIPE#37 White Tea Cucumber Detox

White tea contains small amounts of theine (enough to make you feel more energized without making you feel nervous) and, as already mentioned in the previous recipe, huge amounts of natural antioxidants. It also brings an interesting flavor to your spa water recipes!

SERVES-5

INGREDIENTS

- 1 cup of white tea (use 2 teabags)
- 1 cucumber, sliced (no need to peel)
- Juice of 1 lemon
- A few fresh rosemary leaves
- Half cup of sliced strawberries
- 1 liter of water

INSTRUCTIONS

1. Using a jar/ water pitcher or container, mix water with white tea.
2. Add cucumber slices, strawberries, rosemary, and lemon juice.
3. Stir, press, cover, and put in a fridge for about 1 hour.
4. Serve chilled, add organic honey to taste if you wish. Don't forget about ice cubes! You know the game!

RECIPE#38 Spinach is Awesome!

What's the most amazing thing about this recipe (aside from health benefits of course)? Its color, yes!

SERVES-5

INGREDIENTS

- half cup of fresh spinach juice (you can also use any healthy, organic green powders of your choice, if pressed for time)
- 1 liter of water
- 1 cucumber, sliced
- 3 kiwi, sliced
- A few fresh mint leaves
- Stevia to sweeten, optional

INSTRUCTIONS

1. Using a jar/ water pitcher or container, mix spinach juice with water.
2. Add cucumber and kiwi slices.
3. Spice up with some fresh mint leaves.
4. Stir and press. Place in a fridge for about 1 hour.
5. Serve chilled with ice cubes. Stir well before serving!
6. My suggestion as for ice cubes—make them green as well, you may want to use some kiwis!

RECIPE#39 Bilberry Weight Loss Team

Have you ever tried bilberry tea? It's a great natural weight loss remedy.

It also helps reduce food cravings. Additional health benefit is that it is packed with Vitamin C and antioxidants. Hence, strong immune system and beautiful skin.

This recipe enhances the amazing benefits of bilberry infusion even more!

SERVES-6

INGREDIENTS

- 1 liter of water
- 1 cup of bilberry infusion (use 1-2 teabags)
- 1 cup of aloe vera water
- 2 grapefruits ,sliced
- ¼ cup of dried mint

INSTRUCTIONS

1. Using a jar/ water pitcher or container, mix water, bilberry infusion, and aloe vera water.
2. Add grapefruits and mint.
3. Stir and press the ingredients slightly.
4. Put in a fridge for about 1 hour.
5. Spice up with some ice cubes if you want.
6. Enjoy!

RECIPE#40 Hibiscus Spa Water for Weight Loss

Here comes another delicious weight loss booster!

SERVES-4

INGREDIENTS

- 1 liter of water
- 2 limes, sliced
- ¼ cup of dried hibiscus flowers
- A few mint leaves
- ½ cup of strawberries (sliced)

INSTRUCTIONS

1. Using a jar/ water pitcher or container, mix water with limes, strawberries, mint, and hibiscus.
2. Stir gently. Press strawberries and limes a bit.
3. Place in a fridge for minimum 1 hour.
4. Serve chilled and add some ice if you wish.
5. Enjoy!

RECIPE#41 Green Tea Made Sweet

Even if you can't stand the taste of green tea, you will love this recipe!

Green tea will make you feel slightly energized and "high". It is also a great natural fat burner.

SERVES-5

INGREDIENTS

- 1 cup of green tea (I like to make it strong)
- 1 liter of water
- 2 tablespoons of honey
- 2 peaches, sliced
- 2 oranges, sliced
- Some ice cubes to spice up

INSTRUCTIONS

1. Using a jar/ water pitcher or container, mix water with green tea.
2. Add 2 tablespoons of honey and orange and peach slices.
3. Stir and press. Cover and store in a fridge for at least one hour.
4. Add some ice cubes for special effect!

RECIPE#42 Moroccan Spa Mix

Moroccan tea is a mix of green tea and fresh mint. It is a soft stimulant that is a much healthier alternative than coffee. Let's mix it with our fruit spa water!

SERVES-6

INGREDIENTS

- 1 cup of green tea, super strong
- 1 cup of mint tea, super strong
- 1 liter of water
- 1 lime, sliced
- 2 lemons, sliced
- 2 peaches, sliced
- ¼ cup of dried mint
- 2 tablespoons of organic honey

INSTRUCTIONS

1. Using a jar/ water pitcher or container, mix green tea with mint tea and water.
2. Add fruits and mint. Sweeten with honey. Stir.
3. Press the fruits a bit and cover.
4. Place in fridge for about 1 hour.
5. Serve chilled, with some fresh mint to garnish, and add a few ice cubes.

RECIPE#43 Echinacea Super Strength Water

When I was a kid, my mum would make me Echinacea infusions or give me Echinacea extract drops on a tablespoon of honey or cane sugar. I was always looking forward to it, in fact, Echinacea was like a special treat to me!

If you want to strengthen your immune system and prevent colds, I strongly suggest regular intake of Echinacea. The end of summer is a good time to start thinking about preventing autumn and winter colds...

SERVES-5

INGREDIENTS

- 1 cup of Echinacea infusion (make it strong, 2 tea bags per cup is fine)
- 1 liter of water
- 2 lemons, sliced
- 1 tablespoon of organic honey
- 1 big red apple, sliced (remove seeds)

INSTRUCTIONS

1. Using a jar/ water pitcher or container, mix water with Echinacea infusion.
2. Add lemons and apple slices.
3. Add honey and stir.
4. Press fruits with a spoon. Cover and cool down in a fridge.
5. Enjoy!

RECIPE#44 Eucalyptus Infusion Water

I recommend this water to everyone suffering from colds, flu, or cough. Of course, don't serve it chilled if you have a sore throat!

Hydration is really important in stimulating your immune system and getting rid of toxins. It stimulates your lymphatic system, which is responsible for getting rid of bacteria.

SERVES-5

INGREDIENTS

- 1 liter of water
- 1 cup of eucalyptus infusion (use 2 teabags per cup to make it stronger)
- A few thyme leaves
- A few mint leaves
- 2 oranges, sliced

INSTRUCTIONS

1. Using a jar/ water pitcher or container, mix water with eucalyptus infusion.
2. Add mint, thyme and orange slices.
3. Cover and set aside for at least a few hours, so that the herbs infuse better.
4. Enjoy!

OPTIONAL: you can serve it chilled and with ice cubes.

RECIPE #45 Strawberry and Thyme Spa Water

Here comes a really easy recipe. All you need are some strawberries and thyme! I love the mix of these two!

SERVES-4

INGREDIENTS

- 1 liter of water
- 1 cup of strawberries, sliced
- 2 tablespoons of thyme
- A few ice cubes (I like blueberry ice cubes with this one, you can also use frozen blueberries, they will serve as ice cubes).

INSTRUCTIONS

1. Using a jar/ water pitcher or container, mix water with strawberries.
2. Add some thyme.
3. Let cool down for a few hours.
4. Add frozen blueberries or other ice cubes of your choice.
5. Enjoy!

RECIPE#46 Polish Kompot Inspired Spa Water (Apples)

This recipe is inspired by traditional Polish fruit infused water called "kompot". Apples are really popular Polish kompot ingredients, but there are also pears, cherries, strawberries, and many more.

SERVES-4, 5

INGREDIENTS

- 1 liter of water
- 5 big apples
- Juice of 2 lemons
- 2 tablespoons of organic honey
- 1 teaspoon of cinnamon
- 1 teaspoon of clove powder

INSTRUCTIONS

1. Bring the water to boil.
2. In the meantime, wash and peel the apples. Cut in small chunks and remove the seeds.
3. The water should be warm, but not boiling. Throw in the apples and add the rest of the ingredients. Stir and cover.
4. Set aside for a few hours or put in a fridge, you can serve it chilled or natural. It is an excellent dessert!

RECIPE#47 Cucumber & Celery Detox

Don't even think of rejecting this recipe before you actually try it. It may look a bit weird, but it's really healthy and fantastic to complement any detox program!

SERVES-8

INGREDIENTS

- 2 liters of water
- 2 cucumbers, sliced
- ¼ cup of diced ginger
- 2 garlic cloves, remove skin
- 4 small celery sticks, with leaves
- 1 peach, sliced
- 2 tablespoons of citrus blossoms flowers (optional)

INSTRUCTIONS

1. Using a jar/ water pitcher or container, mix water with cucumbers, ginger, garlic, celery sticks, and peach slices.
2. Throw in some citrus blossoms flowers.
3. Stir, press, and cover.
4. Let infuse for a few hours, or, for maximum flavor and detox effects, leave overnight.
5. Enjoy!

RECIPE#48 Lavender Vanilla Citrus Dream

This recipe will make you love lemons and limes! If needed, use stevia, honey or maple syrup to sweeten.

SERVES-8

INGREDIENTS

- 2 liters of water
- 2 teaspoons of vanilla extract
- 2 tablespoons of dried lavender
- 2 limes, sliced
- 2 lemons, sliced
- Stevia, maple syrup or honey to sweeten, if needed

INSTRUCTIONS

1. Using a jar/ water pitcher or container, mix water with lime and lemon slices.
2. Add vanilla extract and dried lavender.
3. Stir and cover. Place in a fridge and let it cool down and infuse for a couple of hours.
4. Serve chilled and feel free to spice it up with ice cubes (blueberry ice cubes or orange juice ice cubes would be great for this one!).
5. Enjoy!

RECIPE#49 Vanilla Beach-Peach Spa

I love the sweet vanilla flavor that this spa water brings!

SERVES-4

INGREDIENTS

- 2 peaches, sliced
- 1 carrot, sliced
- 1 liter of water
- ¼ cup of fresh mint
- 1 teaspoon of natural vanilla extract

INSTRUCTIONS

1. Using a jar/ water pitcher or container, mix water with peaches and carrot slices.
2. Add mint and vanilla.
3. Cover and let cool down and infuse in a fridge for a couple of hours.

RECIPE#50 Melon Spa Water with a Twist

Melon mixed with spices and basil turns plain, boring water into an unforgettable, exotic and refreshing experience!

SERVES-4

INGREDIENTS

- 2 tablespoons of basil leaves (fresh)
- 4 melon slices, chunked
- 1 teaspoon of allspice
- 2 cinnamon sticks
- 1 liter of water

INSTRUCTIONS

1. Using a jar/ water pitcher or container, mix water with lemon, basil, allspice, and cinnamon sticks.
2. Stir and press.
3. Cover and place in a fridge for a few hours, so that the herbs infuse more.
4. Serve chilled, with ice cubes. Enjoy!

RECIPE #51 Kiwi Cilantro Mix

Kiwi and cilantro are a simple, refreshing and very powerful blend. The main bonus here is that this recipe is super easy!

SERVES-4

INGREDIENTS

- 2 kiwis, peeled and sliced
- 2 tablespoons of cilantro
- 1 liter of water
- Optional: a few lime slices

INSTRUCTIONS

1. Using a jar/ water pitcher or container, mix water with kiwis and cilantro.
2. Press the kiwis a bit with a spatula.
3. Set aside in a fridge for a few hours. That way, you will be able to enjoy the maximum flavors. Cilantro may take a few hours to infuse at its best.
4. Add some ice cubes if you wish, enjoy!

RECIPE#52 Carrot Summer Mix

I know what you are thinking...are carrots part of fruit infused water ingredients?

I say—if not, why not? Try it yourself!

SERVES-4

INGREDIENTS

- 2 carrots, peeled and sliced
- 2 apples, sliced
- 1 lime, sliced
- 2 tablespoons of dried rose flowers
- 1 liter of water
- Ice cubes

INSTRUCTIONS

1. Using a jar/ water pitcher or container, mix water with carrots, apples, and limes.
2. Add rose flowers.
3. Stir and press.
4. Let infuse for at least 1 hour. Rose flowers will give it an incredible taste. Make sure that the flowers are pesticide free.
5. Serve with ice cubes of your choice! Enjoy!

What is your favorite recipe? Please let me know by posting a review. I would love to hear from you!

CONCLUSION

I hope I was able to inspire you and help you get started on preparing your own spa water. Your HOLISTIC wellness success is just round the corner! Use your imagination and feel free to experiment. Create your own luxurious health SPA at home and make your family and friends hooked on it!

And remember...when you finish your spa water, you can always re-fill the jar. Of course, the flavor won't be as strong as the first jar, but you can always spice it up with some fresh lemon or lime juice and mint. Plus, it is a wonderful solution if you are pressed for time or are having some guests over.

Don't throw away the fruits from your recipes. Eat them after finishing your spa water (or when drinking your spa water, it's up to you!). You can also use them for desserts, smoothies, cakes and ice-cream.

"Vitaminize" it UP this summer and all year long!

****

Until next time we "meet", I wish you all the best on your wellness quest,

Much love,

Marta

Your friend and motivator in holistic self-care

Conclusion

Made in the USA
Las Vegas, NV
09 March 2022

45312438R00046